MW00388488

Drum Styles
Book with Audio Access

by
Tim Wimer

For Free Online Audio Access
Go to this address on the internet:

http://cvls.com/extras/ds/

A SPECIAL THANKS TO

Bert Casey and Geoff Hohwald for their production assistance and dedication to this project.

Robert Chernault and Noteworthy Music for providing instruments and accessories for photographs, as well as encouragement.

Ken Rattenbury and Fret Mill Music for giving me an opportunity to learn through teaching.

Matt Stewart for helping with the photographs.

Kevin Hurley for the cover photo.

Jeremy Price for helping to compile the Artist and Album lists.

My wife, Funda, for her encouragement during my projects.

DEDICATION

This book is dedicated to my mom. Thanks for lugging my drum set to elementary school for band concerts.

INTRODUCTION

Learning to play drums means learning to play many styles of music. By classifying yourself as a "rock drummer" or a "jazz drummer," you limit yourself as an artist, and ultimately as a working musician. On any given job, you may be expected to provide solid and interesting rhythms for a variety of musical styles. As a rhythmic chef, you have to know many musical recipes.

This book is designed to provide the student with knowledge of many musical styles, including rock, reggae, blues, latin, and jazz. After working through these chapters, you will be able to play thousands of songs based on these styles. The order in which you cover the chapters is not important. It should be noted, however, that the exercises in each chapter are progressive, beginning with the easiest and working toward the most difficult.

The Audio Tracks which accompanies this book will enable the student to learn 3 or 4 times faster. The Audio Tracks allow the student to hear the accent, tone, and rhythm of the musical examples included in the book. It should take the average student several months to complete this material. Don't be in a hurry. Take your time and enjoy exploring the many exciting styles of drumming.

THE AUTHOR

Tim Wimer began drumming during the late 1970's in his school band program. Since then, he has played in rock, pop, country, jazz, blues, and orchestral bands, including the 82nd Airborne Division Band where he served as a paratrooper and musician. He currently lives in Roanoke, Virginia, where he teaches privately and works with school band programs. Tim has also written two other books, *The Drum Primer & 10 Lessons In Rudiments & Rhythms,* as well as two DVDs, *Introduction to Drums & Snare Drum Rudiments.*

LET US KNOW WHAT YOU THINK

Hundreds of hours were spent developing this method based on experience with teaching students. Our goal is to provide high quality material at a reasonable price and we constantly improve the product based on your needs. We are concerned that these books are useful and valuable to your progress as a drummer. Send any comments or suggestions regarding our books and DVDs to:

Watch & Learn, Inc.
1882 Queens Way
Atlanta, GA 30341
800-416-7088

TABLE OF CONTENTS

MUSICAL TERMS & SIGNS

TERMS & SIGNS

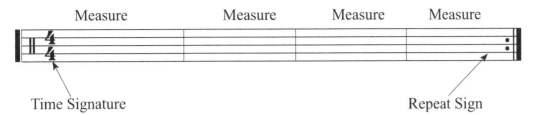

Measure   Measure   Measure   Measure

Time Signature   Repeat Sign

A **measure** is a subdivision within a line. Four measures are shown above.

A **time signature** is a fractional number which tells you how many beats can fit into each measure. The top number tells how many beats each measure holds, while the bottom number tells what type of note equals one beat. In 4/4 time, four quarter notes will fit into each measure. In 3/4 time, three quarter notes will fit into each measure. In 6/8 time, six eighth notes will fit into each measure.

A **repeat sign** indicates that you should repeat a previous passage or measure.

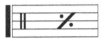   This sign means to repeat the previous measure.

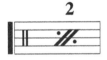   This sign means to repeat the previous two measures.

DYNAMICS

Dynamics refers to volume. The following markings indicate how loudly or softly to play.

fff	Very, very loud	
ff	Very loud	A crescendo indicates a gradual increase in volume
f	Loud	
mf	Medium loud	
mp	Medium soft	
p	Soft	A decrescendo indicates a gradual decrease in volume.
pp	Very soft	
ppp	Very, very soft	

1

NOTATION CHART

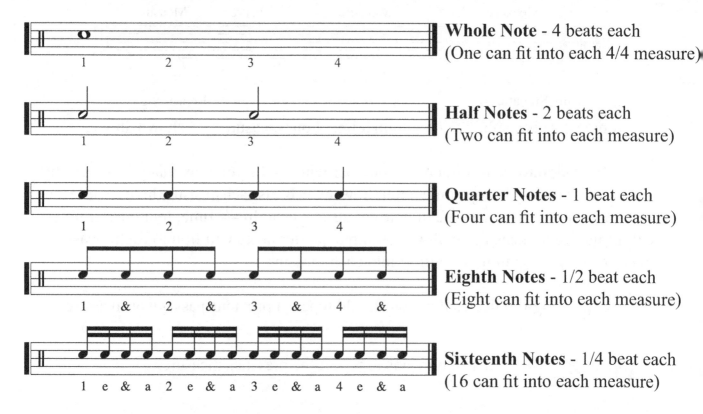

Whole Note - 4 beats each
(One can fit into each 4/4 measure)

Half Notes - 2 beats each
(Two can fit into each measure)

Quarter Notes - 1 beat each
(Four can fit into each measure)

Eighth Notes - 1/2 beat each
(Eight can fit into each measure)

Sixteenth Notes - 1/4 beat each
(16 can fit into each measure)

More advanced rhythms can be created by removing a note (or notes) from a group of 4 sixteenth notes. These rhythms can be written with a sixteenth note rest, or as an eighth - sixteenth note combination.

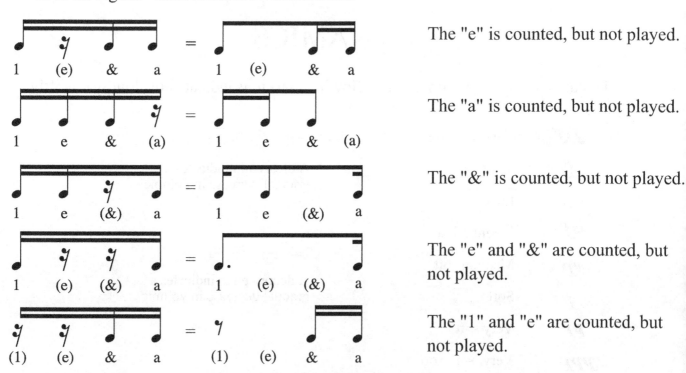

The "e" is counted, but not played.

The "a" is counted, but not played.

The "&" is counted, but not played.

The "e" and "&" are counted, but not played.

The "1" and "e" are counted, but not played.

2

TRIPLETS

A triplet is a group of 3 notes which are played evenly.

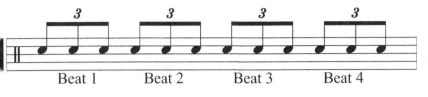

Eighth Note Triplets
Each set of 3 equals 1 beat
(4 sets can fit into each 4/4 measure)

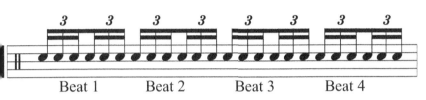

Sixteenth Note Triplets
Each set of 3 equals 1/2 beat
(8 sets of 3 can fit into each 4/4 measure)

RESTS

Rests tell how many beats not to play.

Whole note rest = 4 beats each

Half note rest = 2 beats each

Quarter note rest = 1 beat each

Eighth note rest = 1/2 beat each

Sixteenth note rest = 1/4 beat each

3

NOTATION KEY

Hi Hat Cymbal

Open Hi Hat

Ride Cymbal

Crash Cymbal

Hi Hat Pedal (with foot)

Snare Drum

Bass Drum

Hi Tom

Medium Tom

Floor Tom

CHAPTER 1
ROCK & ROLL

NOTABLE NAMES IN ROCK DRUMMING

We have included some of the most notable players, past and present, in the rock scene. By listening to these drummers, you will become more familiar with the flavor of rock drumming as it is applied to songs.

Drummer	Group	Album
Ringo Starr	Beatles	A Hard Day's Night
John Bonham	Led Zeppelin	Four
Keith Moon	The Who	Who's Next
Charlie Watts	Rolling Stones	Paint It Blue
Ginger Baker	Cream	Strange Brew
Carl Palmer	Emerson, Lake, & Palmer	Brain Salad Surgery
Bill Bruford	Yes	Fragile
Neil Peart	Rush	Moving Pictures
Stewart Copeland	The Police	Synchronicity
Alex Van Halen	Van Halen	1984
Mike Portnoy	Dream Theatre	Images and Words
Lars Ulrich	Metallica	And Justice For All
Terry Bozzio	Jeff Beck	Guitar Shop
Greg Bissonette	Joe Satriani	The Extremist
Tim Alexander	Primus	Sailing the Seas of Cheese
Vinnie Colaiuta	Sting	Ten Summoner's Tales
Carter Beauford	Dave Matthews	Remember Two Things
Chad Smith	Red Hot Chili Peppers	One Hot Minute
Kenny Aronoff	John Mellencamp	All

ROCK & ROLL

Rock Drumming can be divided into four main categories:
1. Quarter note beats
2. Eighth note beats
3. One handed sixteenth note beats
4. Two handed sixteenth note beats

Although the snare drum and bass drum parts may be similar throughout these four sub-styles, the hi hat variations produce different sounding beats. Most rock & roll songs are played in 4/4 time (each measure gets 4 beats). This chapter will offer many examples of 4/4 beats spanning the four sub-styles.

QUARTER NOTES ON THE CYMBAL

Playing quarter notes on the hi hat or ride cymbal is an effective way to play fast songs or to add drive. This style of drumming can be heard in such songs as Tom Petty's *American Girl*, Nirvana's *All Apologies,* and Steppenwolf's *Born To Be Wild.*

At first, playing steady quarter notes on the hi hat cymbal may appear to be easy. But as the bass drum and snare drum parts become more difficult, so too does playing steady quarter notes on the cymbal. You will most likely find that your right hand will want to play with the snare and bass drum, rather than work independently. As you work through the following exercises, play them slowly until you have mastered the beat, then gradually increase the tempo to a more practical speed. You may wish to crack the hi hat cymbals slightly by releasing pressure with the foot. This will create a heavier sound. Using the bell of the ride cymbal can also offer a heavier effect.

To create the most basic quarter note beat, begin by playing quarter notes on the hi hat or ride cymbal with the right stick. These notes will be counted 1 2 3 4.

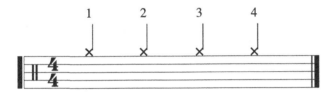

Now add the snare drum to beats 2 and 4 with the left stick.

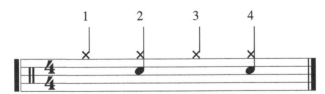

Add the bass drum to beats 1 and 3.

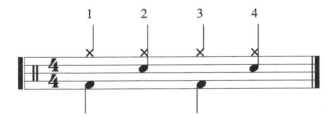

QUARTER NOTE BEATS

EIGHTH NOTES ON THE CYMBAL

The majority of rock songs use eighth notes on the hi hat or ride cymbal. This style of drumming can be heard on such songs as ZZ Top's *Sharp Dressed Man*, Led Zeppelin's *Stairway to Heaven*, and Neil Young's *Rocking in the Free World*, to name only a few.

Basic eighth note beats do not require a lot of independence skills, since the bass and snare notes are accompanied by a cymbal note. However, beats that incorporate eighth - sixteenth note combinations on the snare and bass, as in the advanced exercises, require a more independent right hand.

To create the most basic eighth note beat, begin by playing eighth notes on the hi hat or ride cymbal. These notes will be counted 1 & 2 & 3 & 4 &.

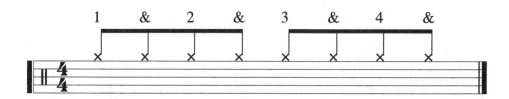

Next add the snare drum (with the left stick) to beats 2 and 4.

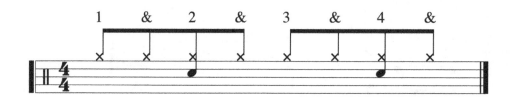

Now add the bass drum to beats 1 and 3.

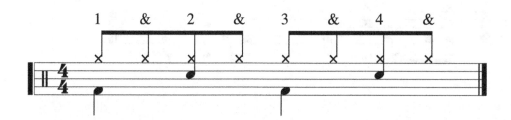

BASIC EIGHTH NOTE BEATS

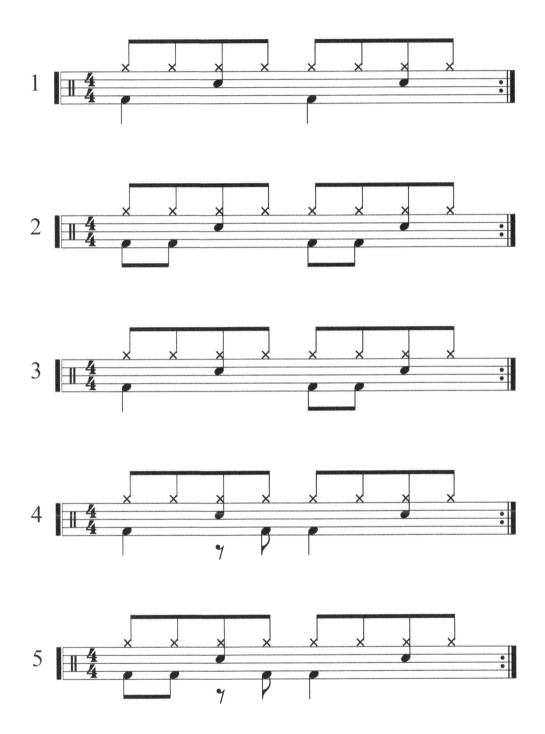

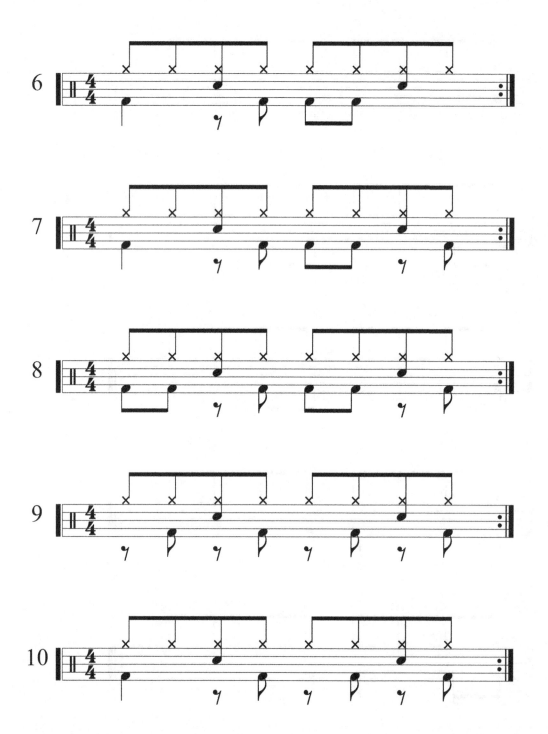

ADVANCED EIGHTH NOTE BEATS

These more advanced exercises incorporate eighth - sixteenth note combinations, as well as open hi hats. You should concentrate on the basic rhythms before attempting to add the open hi hats.

ONE HANDED SIXTEENTH NOTES

In this section, you will learn beats which use sixteenth notes that are played on the cymbal (ride or hi hat) with the right hand. Songs that use this type of beat are typically slower, since there is a limit to how fast sixteenth notes can be played steadily using only one hand. Examples of this style can be heard in such songs as Rush's *Tom Sawyer*, Bad Company's *Ready For Love,* and Ted Nugent's *Strangle Hold.*

To create the most basic one handed sixteenth note beat, begin by playing sixteenth notes on the hi hat or ride cymbal with the right stick. These notes are counted 1 e & a 2 e & a 3 e & a 4 e & a.

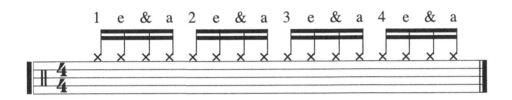

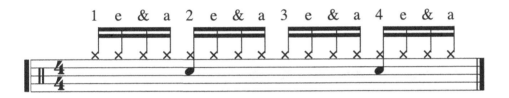

ONE HANDED SIXTEENTH NOTE BEATS

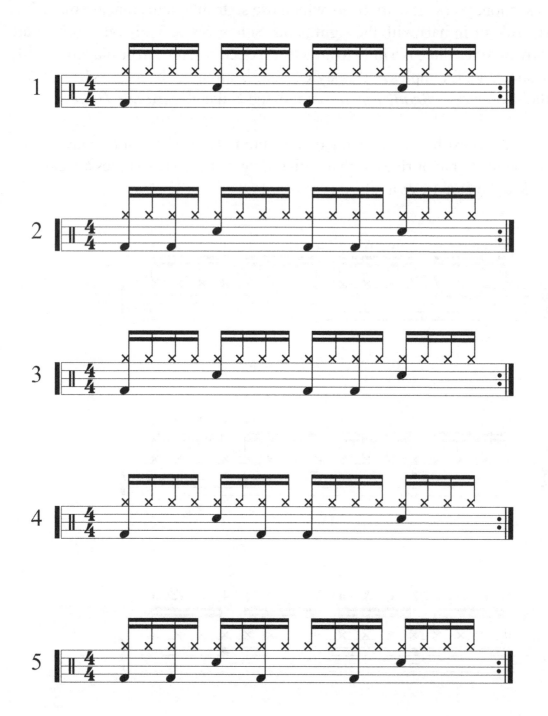

Exercises 6 - 10 incorporate open hi hats. You should first concentrate on playing the basic rhythms, then add the open hi hats.

TWO HANDED SIXTEENTH NOTES

This style of drumming is used in many pop and rock tunes, such as *Only Want to Be With You* by Hootie and the Blowfish and *Smoke on the Water* by Deep Purple.

Speed is the most practical reason for using both hands to play sixteenth notes on the hi hat cymbal. By alternating your right and left sticks on the hi hat, you will greatly increase your speed. It is especially important to practice these beats slowly at first to ensure that you are using the proper sticking. Once the beat is mastered at a slow tempo, it is much easier to speed it up.

To create the most basic two handed sixteenth note beat, begin by playing sixteenth notes on the hi hat. The sticking should be R L R L throughout.

The snare drum will be added to beats 2 and 4. Notice that the hi hat does not play with the snare drum. Immediately after the snare is struck, the left stick resumes on the hi hat. (More advanced beats may require the snare to be played with the left stick).

Now add the bass drum to beats 1 and 3. Note that the bass will be playing while the right stick is striking the hi hat. (More advanced beats may require the bass to play while the left stick is striking the hi hat).

TWO HANDED SIXTEENTH NOTE BEATS

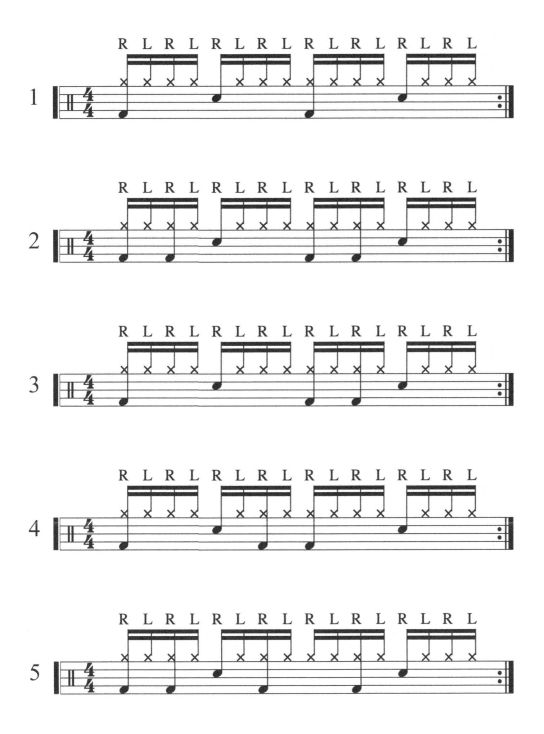

6

7

8

9

10

ROCK FILLS

Drum fills are used to add excitement to songs and to emphasize particular parts. The following drum fills should be practiced in the context of a four bar phrase, meaning that a beat is played for 3 measures, then the fill is played as the 4th measure. Immediately after the fill, you should begin the beat again. Stickings are provided to make drum to drum transitions more natural.

Now let's apply what you have learned in this chapter as we play along with a full band on the Audio Tracks. This song example uses quarter, eighth, and two handed sixteenth notes on the cymbal.

SONG 1 - ROCK & ROLL

EQUIPMENT SPOTLIGHT

DOUBLE BASS PEDAL

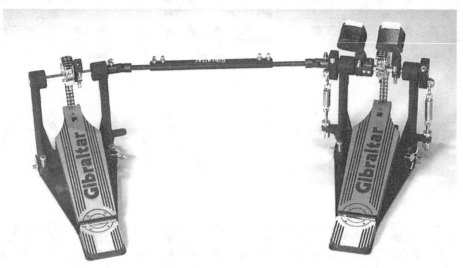

How can you make it sound like you have two bass drums when you only have one? It's simple. Buy a double pedal. The left pedal controls the left beater, while the right pedal controls the right beater. Both beaters strike a single bass drum, allowing you to create some exciting double bass effects.

CHINA & SPLASH CYMBALS

Various cymbals can add new dimensions to your sound. A china cymbal (left) is a cross between a crash cymbal and a gong. It produces a heavy and sustained sound. It can also provide a unique appearance to your setup.

A splash cymbal (right) is designed for a quick attack with little sustain, making it ideal for selected accents.

BOOM STANDS

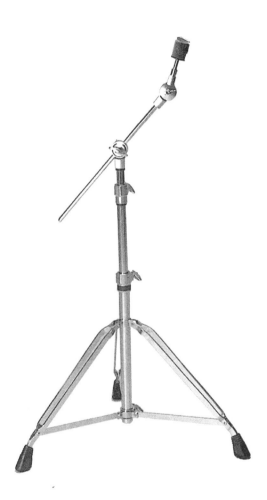

Boom stands can allow you to get your cymbals in just the right spot. In addition to moving vertically, the boom arm may also be adjusted laterally and diagonally. This accessory can help prevent needless frustration.

ROTO TOMS

Roto Toms are a great way to add three more drums to your kit. They produce a high pitched bongo like sound, but are designed to be played with drumsticks, rather than hands. The pitch of these toms can be changed quickly and easily simply by rotating the drums. They truly are unique.

TAMBOURINES

Tambourines are available in many styles. The concert tambourine (left) is characterized by its head, which can be played with the hand or fingers to produce a tone, as well as a jingle. Also, concert tambourines are made of a wooden shell.

Rock tambourines (right) do not have a head, and therefore produce only a jingle. This style is generally played by shaking with the wrist, rather than tapping with the hand. The tambourine pictured is a modified rock tambourine which can be mounted on a stand and incorporated into drumset playing.

STICK BAG

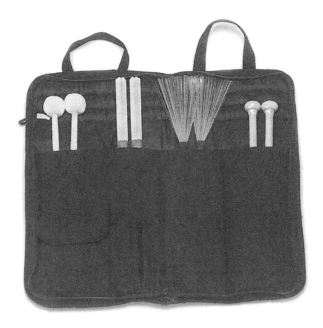

A stick bag is ideal for keeping your sticks, brushes, rods, and mallets in one convenient location. Stick bags are available in nylon or leather.

We have included photographs and descriptions of equipment you may not have seen. Many music stores have these products, so check them out during your next visit. There are additional photos of other percussion instruments on pages 39, 43, 61, and 69.

CHAPTER 2
REGGAE

REGGAE

Reggae first appeared as a musical style in Jamaica during the 1960's. Since then it has influenced much of America's popular music. Great reggae artists include Bob Marley, Ziggy Marley, and Jimmy Cliff.

Reggae songs typically use 4/4 meter, and are often characterized by off beat eighth and sixteenth notes played on the cymbal (along with the guitar).

Begin by playing off beat eighth notes on the hi hat with the right stick.

Next add the snare drum to beats 2 and 4. Using rimknocks (keeping the stick's bead against the head and striking the rim with the butt end) can help provide a more authentic reggae flavor.

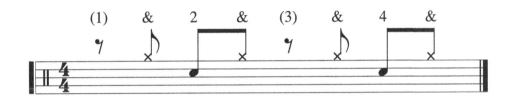

Now add the bass drum to beats 1 and 3.

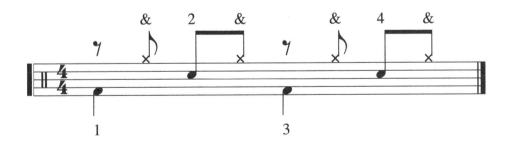

REGGAE BEATS

FUNKY REGGAE

More funky reggae beats can be created by using sixteenth note triplets. Be sure to listen to the audio Tracks to get the proper hi hat rhythm.

Now let's apply what you learned in chapter 2 as we play along with a full band on the Audio Tracks. This song example uses a repetitive two bar pattern. Notice that a different two bar pattern is used for the chorus.

SONG 2 - REGGAE

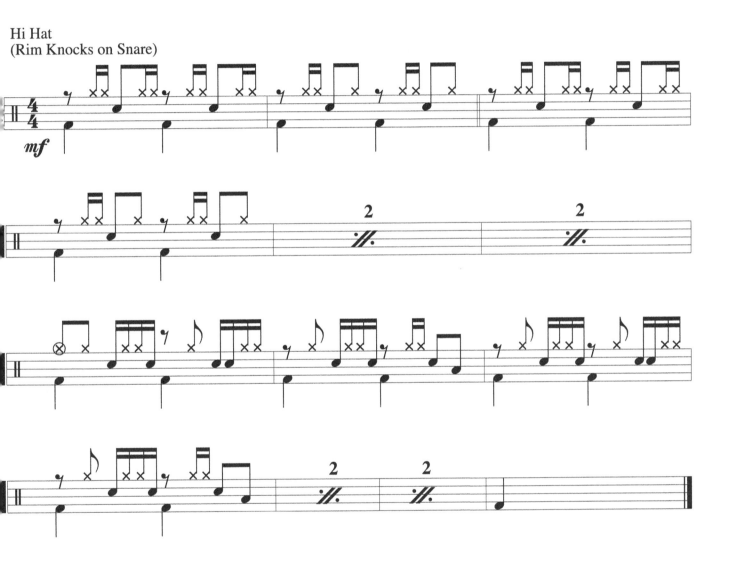

CHAPTER 3
LATIN

LATIN

Whether playing in a rock, pop, or jazz group, at some point you will be required to play latin rhythms. While most latin bands have a percussion section which includes congas, bongos, timbales, and many other percussion instruments, latin rhythms can be adapted to the drum set.

Begin by getting comfortable with the ride cymbal (played with the right stick on the bell) and the bass drum part. Play steady eighth notes on the ride, and beats 1 and 3 on the bass.

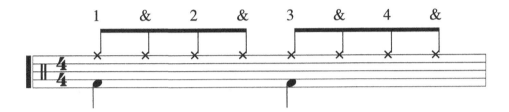

Next, add the hi hat (played with the foot) to beats 2 and 4.

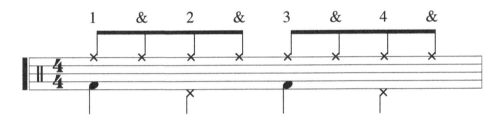

Make sure you can play the ride, bass, and hi hat consistently before attempting to add the snare drum.

The snare parts for latin beats are highly syncopated and are often played as rimknocks (the butt end of the stick will strike the rim while the bead remains on the drum head) which produces a clave sound.

BASIC LATIN BEATS

When practicing the following beats, it may be helpful to practice the ride and snare parts before adding the bass and hi hat.

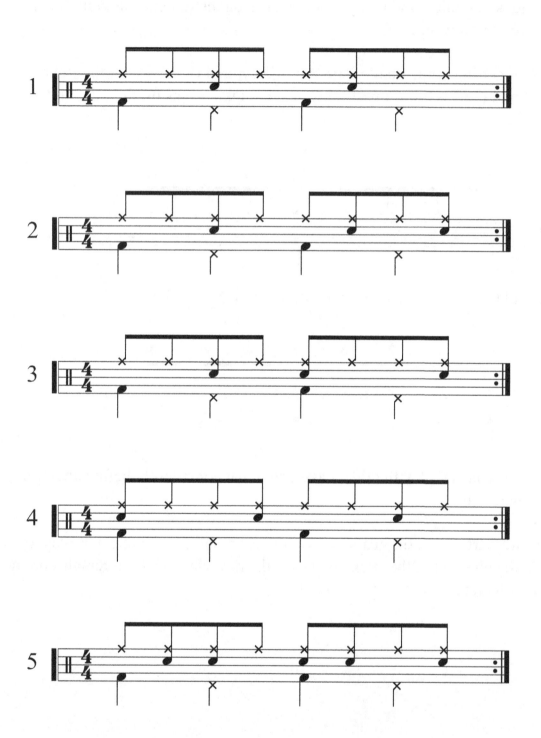

TWO MEASURE COMBINATIONS

ADVANCED LATIN BEATS

We will create more challenging latin rhythms by using a combination of eighth and sixteenth notes on the ride cymbal. It may be helpful to practice the ride cymbal and snare parts together before adding the bass and hi hat.

Now let's apply what you learned in chapter 3 as we play along with a full band on the Audio Tracks. This song example contrasts basic beats (during the verse) with advanced beats (during the chorus).

SONG 3 - LATIN

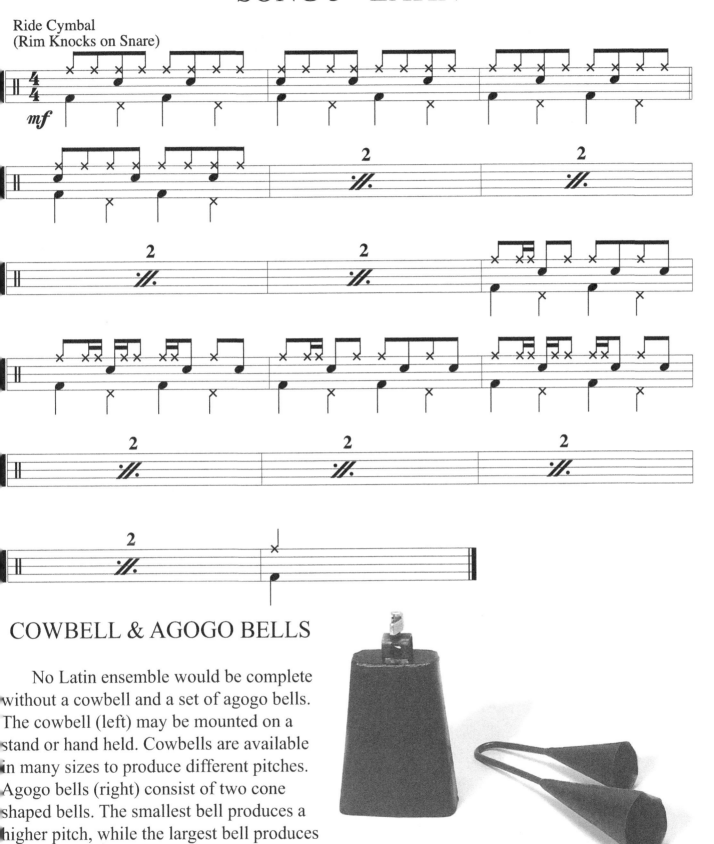

COWBELL & AGOGO BELLS

No Latin ensemble would be complete without a cowbell and a set of agogo bells. The cowbell (left) may be mounted on a stand or hand held. Cowbells are available in many sizes to produce different pitches. Agogo bells (right) consist of two cone shaped bells. The smallest bell produces a higher pitch, while the largest bell produces a lower pitch.

EXTRA CHALLENGE - SAMBA

The samba became popular in Rio de Janeiro during the 1920's. It seems to be more familiar to ball room dancers than to drummers, but because of its rhythmic flavor, it should not be overlooked as a unique style.

Warning - This style of drumming requires excellent independence skills. Be patient and expect some frustration.

Begin by practicing the ride cymbal and bass drum parts. Play steady quarter notes on the ride bell while playing beat 1, the & of 2, 3 and the & of 4 on the bass drum.

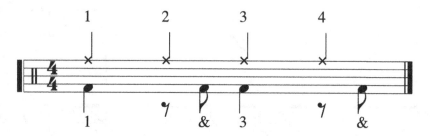

Now add the hi hat (with the left foot) to beats 2 and 4.

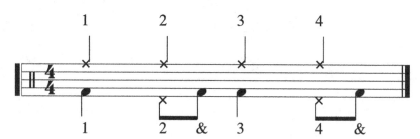

Make sure you are comfortable with the ride, bass, and hi hat parts before attempting to add the snare drum.

SAMBA BEATS

While practicing the following beats, flip the snare drum strainer to the off position to get a tom sound. It may be helpful to get the ride, bass, and hi hat started before attempting to add the snare drum.

SAMBA BEATS

Exercises 6 - 10 incorporate the toms.

BONGO & CONGO DRUMS

Bongo drums (left) and Conga drums (right) are two of the most popular hand drums today. Various bass and slap techniques can be used to produce different sounds and tones. Bongos are commonly sold as a pair, while congas may be sold individually or as a pair. For more information on learning to play hand drums, consult your local music store about books and videos.

MARACAS & EGGS

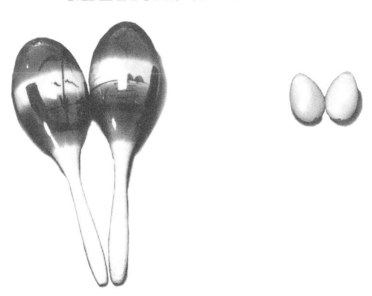

Maracas (left) and eggs (right) are hand held instruments of the shaker family. Maracas typically produce a louder, lower pitched sound, while eggs tend to produce a higher pitched, softer sound. These instruments are usually played by an auxiliary percussionist in a Latin group, but may be incorporated into drum set playing via a free hand.

CHAPTER 4
BLUES

6/8 BLUES

The distinctive sound of 6/8 blues drumming can be heard in George Thorougood's *Bad to the Bone* and such blues classics as *Stormy Monday* and *Mississippi Blues*.

In 6/8 time, six eighth notes can be put into each measure. They will be counted 1 2 3 4 5 6. Sixteenth notes written in 6/8 time are counted 1 & 2 & 3 & 4 & 5 & 6 &. 6/8 beats are not difficult to play once you get comfortable counting in 6, rather than 4 as in 4/4 time.

To create a basic 6/8 blues beat, begin by playing eighth notes on the hi hat (or ride cymbal) with the right stick. They will be counted 1 2 3 4 5 6.

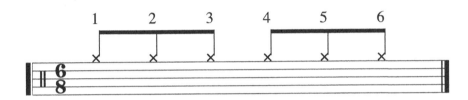

Next, add the snare drum to beat 4 with the left stick.

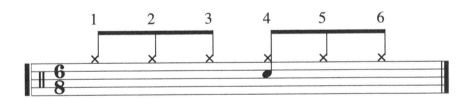

Now complete the beat by adding a bass drum to beat 1.

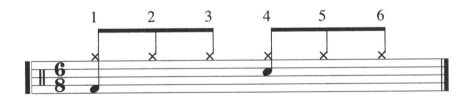

BASIC 6/8 BLUES BEATS

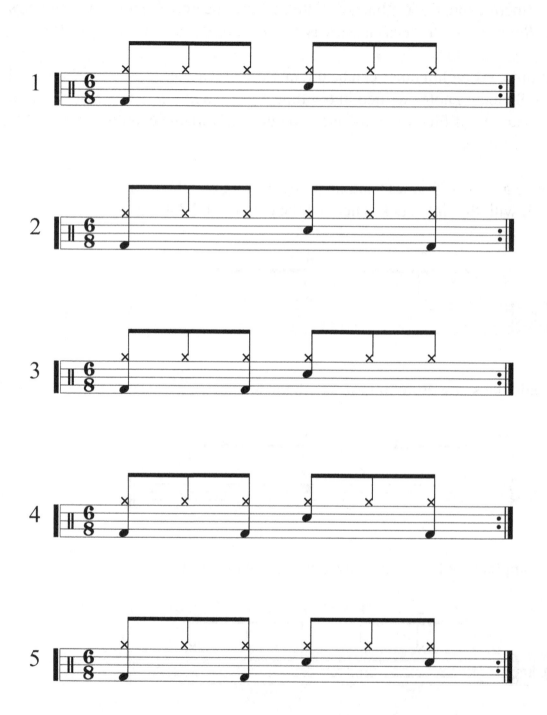

BASIC TWO MEASURE COMBINATIONS

ADVANCED 6/8 BLUES BEATS

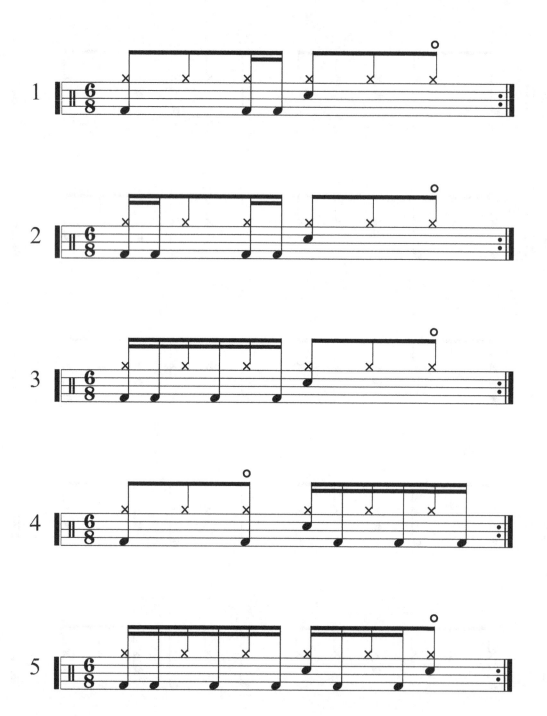

TWO MEASURE COMBINATIONS

6/8 FILLS

After you are comfortable with the following blues fills, practice them as part of a 4 bar phrase, playing a 6/8 beat for three measures and the fill as the fourth measure. Stickings are provided to make drum to drum transitions more natural.

Now let's apply what you learned in this chapter as we play along with a full band on the Audio Tracks. The 24 bar structure of this example is typical of many blues tunes.

SONG 4 - 6/8 BLUES

THE BLUES SHUFFLE

The blues shuffle is typically used for faster blues tunes, such as Stevie Ray Vaughn's *Before You Accuse Me* and the Doors' *Roadhouse Blues*. These beats are characterized by a bouncy hi hat sound.

Shuffle rhythms can be written in 6/8 time, with beats 2 and 5 being rests, as shown below:

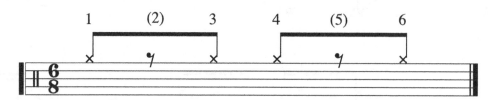

Since shuffle beats are generally set to up tempo songs, it is easier to think of them as eighth note triplets played in 4/4 time. (A triplet is a group of three notes that are played evenly). We will remove the second note from each set of triplets, which will create the bouncy hi hat effect.

Begin by playing the triplet pattern shown below. The notes will be counted Trip - let Trip - let Trip - let Trip - let. (Each Trip - let gets one beat, so four sets make up each measure).

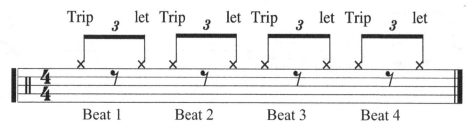

Now add the snare drum to beats 2 and 4 (the 2nd and 4th Trip).

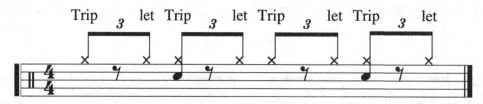

To complete the beat, play the bass drum on beats 1 and 3 (the 1st and 3rd Trip).

SHUFFLE BEATS

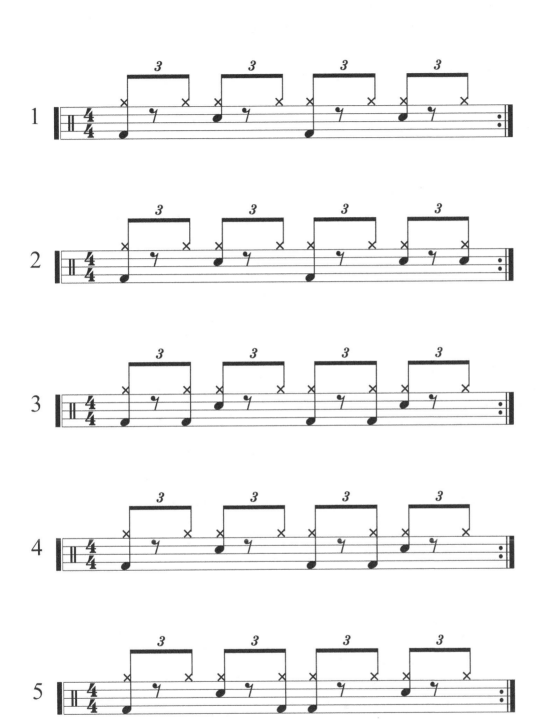

53

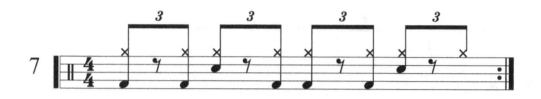

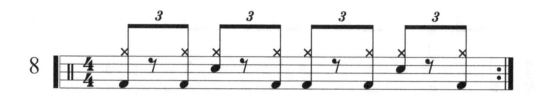

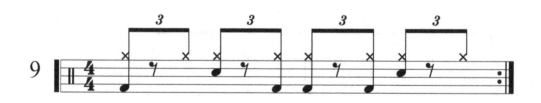

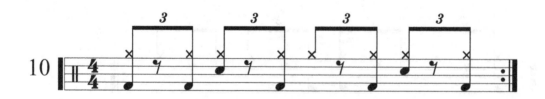

Now let's apply the blues shuffle as we play along with a full band on the Audio Tracks. Although the beat is similar throughout the song, the flavor of the 2nd half is changed by playing the ride cymbal, instead of the hi hat.

SONG 5 - BLUES SHUFFLE

EXTRA CHALLENGE: THE FUNK SHUFFLE

Although it is not commonly used in blues tunes, the funk shuffle does share something in common with the blues shuffle. Like the blues shuffle, the hi hat part is based on a triplet rhythm, with the middle note being a rest. But the funk shuffle has a half time feel, so sixteenth note triplets, rather than eighth note triplets are used.

Begin by playing the hi hat part, which is counted Trip - let   Trip - let. (Note that each set of sixteenth note triplets equals 1 beat).

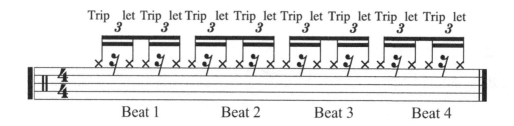

Next, add the snare drum to beats 2 and 4.

Now add the bass drum to beats 1 and 3.

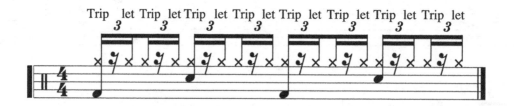

FUNK SHUFFLE BEATS

57

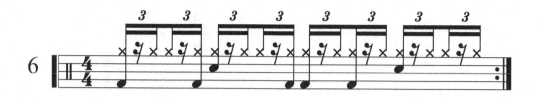

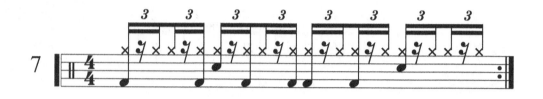

FUNK SHUFFLE FILLS

Like funk shuffle beats, funk shuffle fills are also based on sixteenth note triplet rhythms. These fills should be practiced as part of a four bar phrase. Stickings are provided to make drum to drum transitions more natural.

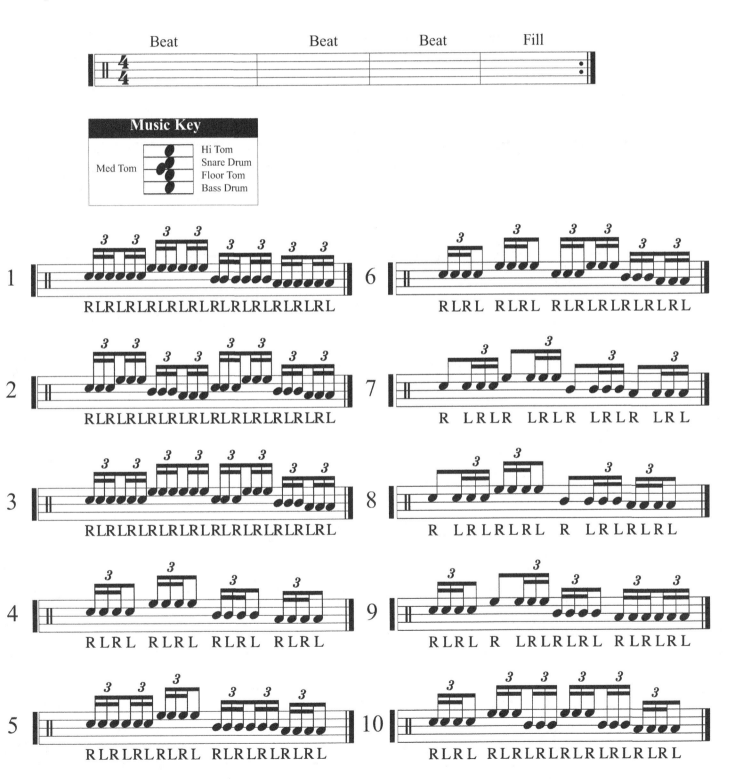

Now let's apply the funk shuffle as we play along with a full band on the Audio Tracks. Remember to keep the beat relaxed and don't rush the tempo.

SONG 6 - FUNK SHUFFLE

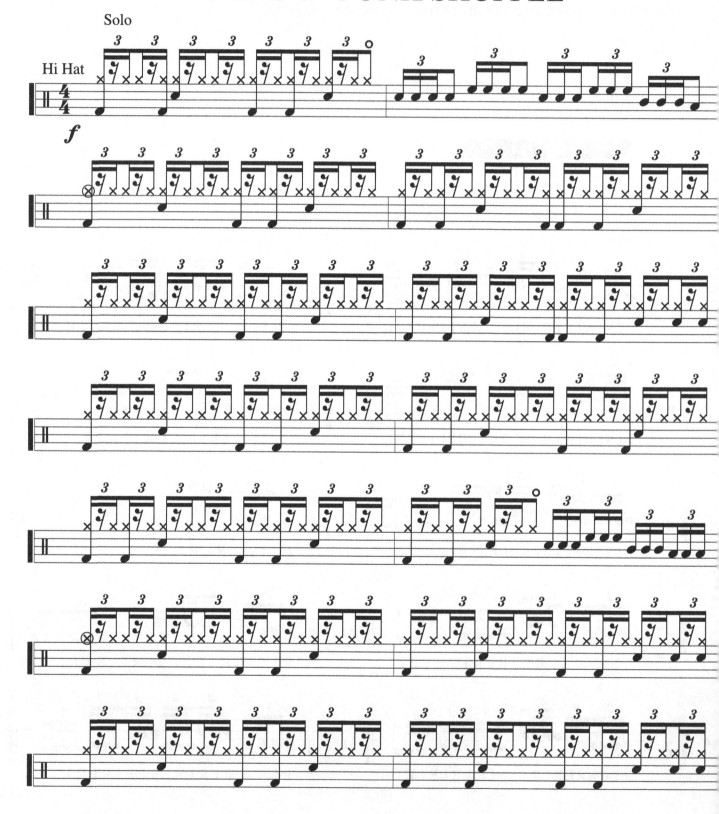

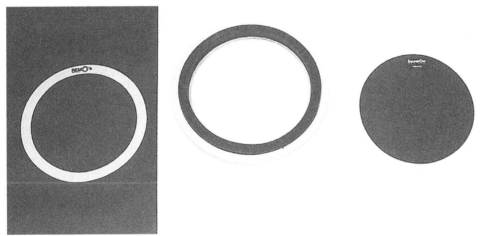

MUFFLING DEVICES

If your drums ring too much for your liking, you may want to invest in muffling devices. Dead Ringers (center) are foam circles which fit inside the drum and muffle the top head. Some dead ringers attach to the shell's lip, while others attach directly to the drum head.

Zero rings (left) lay on the outside of the drum head. They work well for reducing higher frequency ringing, especially on the snare drum. It's amazing what this thin piece of plastic can do to change the sound of a drum.

Silencing pads (right) can allow you to practice without disturbing the neighbors. These foam pads lay on the outside of the head and decrease the drum's volume while still allowing its pitch to be heard. Silencing pads are also available for cymbals.

CHAPTER 5
JAZZ

JAZZ

Because they require a lot of independence, jazz beats are among the most challenging to play. While playing jazz, the right hand will play a swing rhythm on the ride cymbal, while the bass drum plays steady quarters. The hi hat accents two and four with the left foot. The snare drum serves as percussive shading, often playing around the two and four pulse, rather than strictly serving as a timekeeper.

Begin by getting comfortable with the ride cymbal rhythm, which uses quarter notes and eighth note triplets (the middle note being a rest). This rhythm is counted 1 Trip - let   3   Trip - let.

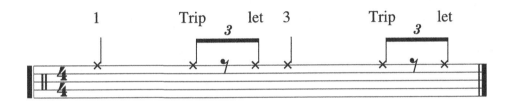

Next, add the bass drum to give a quarter note pulse.

Note - When playing jazz, the bass drum should not be overpowering. Keep the volume low to help the beat flow properly.

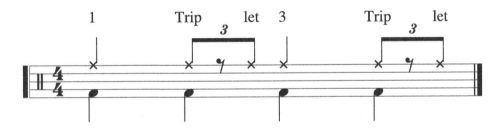

Play beats 2 and 4 with your left foot on the hi hat pedal.

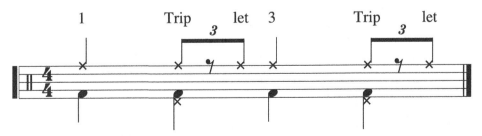

Make sure you are comfortable with the ride, bass, and hi hat parts before you add the snare drum.

BASIC JAZZ BEATS

While learning the following beats, we suggest practicing the ride and snare parts together first, then adding the bass and hi hat.

ADVANCED JAZZ BEATS

Exercises 6 - 10 incorporate accents (>) which make notes louder. Concentrate on playing the basic rhythms first, then work on adding the accent.

JAZZ FILLS

Like jazz beats, jazz fills rely on triplet rhythms. After you are comfortable with the rhythm and sticking of each fill, practice it as part of a four bar phrase, playing a beat for three measures, and the fill as the fourth. Immediately after the fill, you should begin the beat again. Stickings are provided to make drum to drum transitions more natural.

66

SYNCOPATED JAZZ FILLS

Syncopation means "off beat". Incorporating syncopated rhythms into jazz fills can add more swing to a song. The following fills share a similar rhythm and feel, with variations among the snare, toms, and bass drum.

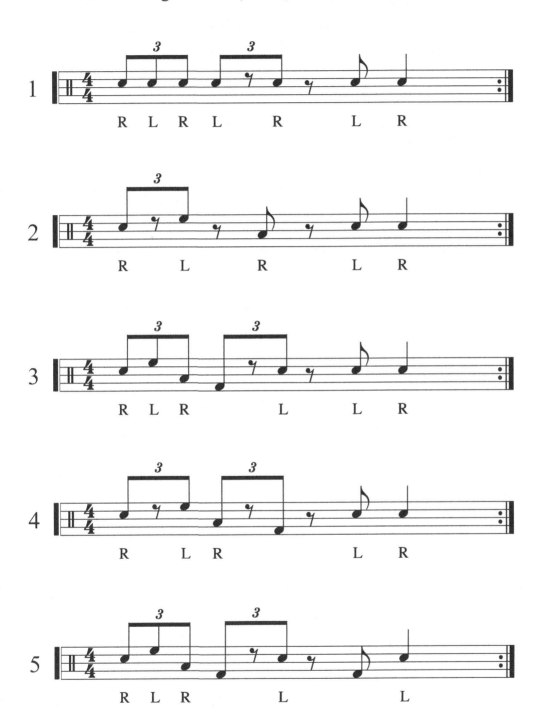

Now let's apply what you have learned in this chapter as we play along with a full band on the Audio Tracks. Be careful not to overpower the music by playing too loud. Keep the beat light and flowing.

SONG 7 - JAZZ

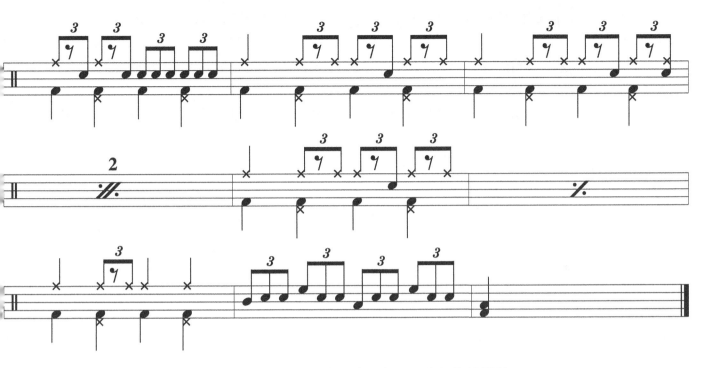

BRUSHES, RODS, & MALLETS

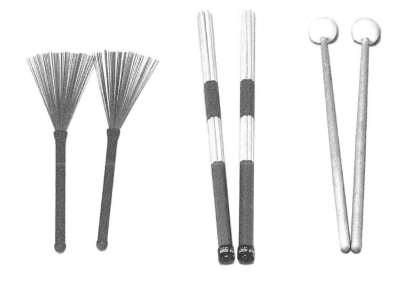

The sound of your kit can be changed by simply using different striking tools. Wire brushes (left) add an interesting texture to the snare drum when swirled around the head. They also produce interesting effects on cymbals. They are much quieter than sticks, making them excellent for playing in small rooms or with unamplified groups. Brushes are also available in nylon, rather than wire.

Wooden rods (center) offer much the same feel as sticks, but produce a different tone and a softer volume. So if your neighbors complain about your practice, get some rods. They are available in different sizes.

Timpani mallets (right) are great for cymbal rolls, which can add intensity to your playing. Mallets are available with hard and soft variations.

EXTRA CHALLENGE - THE JAZZ WALTZ

The jazz waltz is written in 3/4 time, so only three beats will fit into each measure. The ride cymbal rhythm is counted 1   Trip - let   3   1   Trip - let   3. The bass will provide a pulse on beat 1, while the hi hat (played with the foot) accents beats 2 and 3.

Begin by practicing the ride cymbal rhythm.

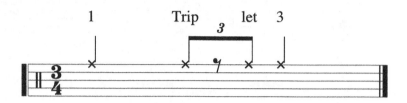

Next, add the bass drum to beat 1.

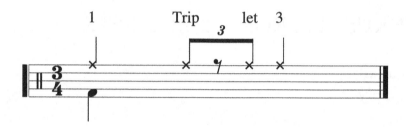

Now add the hi hat (played with the left foot) to beats 2 and 3.

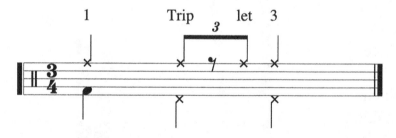

Make sure you are comfortable with the ride, bass, and hi hat rhythms before attempting to add the snare drum.

JAZZ WALTZ BEATS

While learning the following jazz waltz beats, practice the ride and snare parts together before attempting to add the bass and hi hat.

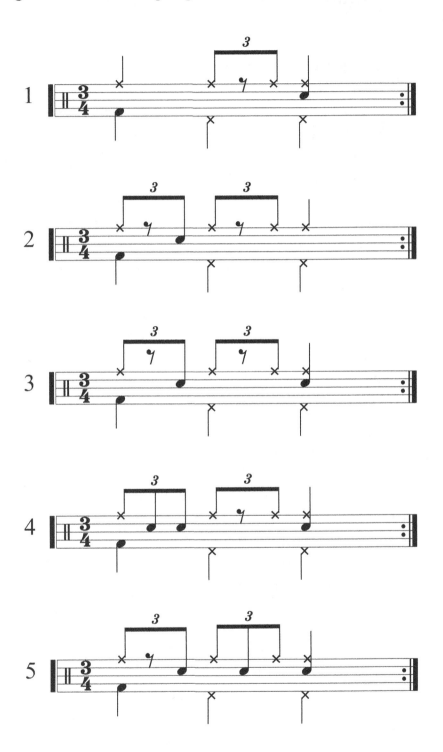

NOTABLE NAMES IN JAZZ

Drummer	Group	Album
Buddy Rich	Buddy Rich	No Jive
Max Roach	Max Roach	+ 4
Tony Williams	Tony Williams	Tokyo
Steve Gadd	Chick Corea	The Leprechaun
Roy Haynes	Roy Haynes	Te Vou!
Elvin Jones	Phineas Newborn	Harlem Blues
Peter Erskine	Jaco Pastorius	The Birthday Concert
Dennis Chambers	John Scofield	Blue Matter
Jack Dejohnette	Jack Dejohnette	Extra Special Edition
Dave Weckl	Dave Weckl	Hardwired
Paul Wertico	Pat Metheny	Letters From Home
Carl Allen	Carl Allen	The Pursuer
Joey Baron	Bill Frisell	Live
Simon Phillips	Simon Phillips	Symbiosis
Art Blakey	Art Blakey & the Jazz Messengers	Orgy In Rhythm

CONCLUSION

I hope you have found this book to be informative and interesting. After you have completed this material, you are ready to move on to the next step, which is learning to apply these styles to music.

While listening to the radio or CDs, try to classify the beats you are hearing, then try to notate them. If you play in a band, experiment with these styles during practice sessions. You will likely discover that by changing the style of beat, you can dramatically change the flavor of a song.

Many volumes could be written on the subject of drum styles, so in order to continue to learn, you should consider several things: first, check out other books and videos. Many are dedicated to exploring one specific style, such as Latin or Jazz. Second, a private instructor can be instrumental in teaching you to apply drum styles, so consult your local music store about lessons.

Thanks for supporting Watch & Learn's products and good luck with your drumming.

GLOSSARY

We have included a glossary of terms that all drummers should know.

Accent Mark (>) - a mark which indicates that a note is to be played louder.

Dynamics - refers to the volume of a song.

Independence - the ability to control the hands and feet independently of each other.

Metronome - a device that keeps a steady beat, allowing musicians to practice time keeping skills.

Ostinado - exercises which combine a repetitive rhythm with two or more limbs while playing an independent rhythm with the remaining limbs.

Polyrhythm - two or more steady rhythms played simultaneously using different limbs.

Rimknock - a clave sound that is created by keeping the stick's bead against the drum head while striking the rim with the stick's butt end.

Rimshot - a high pitched accent which is created by striking the head with the stick's bead while simultaneously striking the rim with the stick's shoulder.

Rudiments - sticking exercises which help develop hand to hand coordination and speed.

Syncopation - refers to off beat rhythms.

Tempo - the speed of a song.

Time Signature - a fractional number which appears at the beginning of a notated song. The top number tells how many beats are in each measure, while the bottom number tells what type of note gets the beat.

Triplet - a group of three notes played evenly.

Made in United States
Orlando, FL
27 October 2023